Alone with God in His Sanctuary

Developing the Ultimate Relationship

Devotional Affirmations
Sanctuary Prayer ~ Sanctuary Journal

Gi Gi Griffin

Alone with God in His Sanctuary
Developing the Ultimate Relationship

by Gi Gi Griffin

ISBN: 978-0-9886824-9-8

Contact Publisher
Griffin Communications
P.O. Box 2906 - Palos Verdes Peninsula, CA 90274
www.inhissanctuary.com

Cover design by Lisa Hainline
www.lionsgatebookdesign.com

Interior design and editing by Edie Glaser
www.craftingstones.com

Acknowledgments

I am deeply grateful to those who have helped me during the writing of this devotional.

Penny Bowles—You are my prayer warrior who believed in me and encouraged me to share my thoughts about our holy Sanctuary within each of us. You have been a huge support to me.

Elizabeth MacDonald—You are my Bible Study teacher and mentor who kept me on track biblically. You are a delight . . . always ready to communicate your godly wisdom to others. You're an inspiration to me.

Jolene Dellenbach—You are a dear friend who was always willing and able to assist when I needed your counsel. I appreciate your warm words and good advice.

Byron MacDonald—You are my Senior Pastor of Rolling Hills Covenant Church. Your love and passion to preach and teach the Bible and to help others come to know God intimately has been an encouragement to me.

Edie Glaser—You are an amazing editor. Your insight into this project has been a tremendous help from start to finish. Your creative abilities go far beyond anything I could have hoped for. Thank you for your meticulous work.

Alfred Griffin—You are my devoted husband. Thank you for your patience and support.

Foreword

I met Gi Gi Griffin in 1981 when she assisted me as a speaker in my early ministry of CLASS (Christian Leaders and Speakers Seminars). I was struck by her beauty and charm. I told everyone that Gi Gi looked as though she had her life all "together," but when she spoke about her involvement in the occult, which eventually led to depression, I knew her life was not as it appeared to be on the outside.

Throughout the years, I have followed Gi Gi's career and am pleased to be asked to write the foreword to her book, *Alone With God In His Sanctuary*. When you pick up this fascinating book you will experience a new world opening up for you.

Alone With God In His Sanctuary describes Gi Gi's spiritual journey from the occult to her alone time with God. Gi Gi has opened her heart to share with you her personal, intimate relationship with God . . . the ultimate relationship!

Florence Littauer
International Speaker and Author

Contents

SECTION II
Affirmations of the Christian Faith

SECTION III
Sanctuary Prayer

SECTION IV
Sanctuary Devotional Journal

". . . God dwells . . . in the gentleness of his Spirit, delighting himself in the tender Christian graces that are budding and blooming all along the peaceful avenues of the soul. Like the gentle south wind blows upon the flowers of the garden and scatters the fragrance; so the Spirit of God fans the heavenly graces implanted in the heart, and a fragrance flows out of the Christian life, awaking admiration in the minds of all who come into his presence."[1]

~ Charles Ebert Orr

Alone with God

When storms of life are round me beating,
When rough the path that I have trod,
Within my closet door retreating,
I love to be alone with God.

Although the clouds have gathered over me
And though I've passed beneath the rod
God's perfect will lies before me,
When I am thus alone with God.

It's there I find new strength for duty,
As over the sands of time I plod
I see the King in all His beauty,
While resting there alone with God.

And when I see the moment nearing
When I shall sleep beneath the sod,
When time with me is disappearing,
I want to be alone with God.

REFRAIN

Alone with God, the world forbidden,
Alone with God, O blessed retreat!
Alone with God, and in Him hidden,
To hold with Him communion sweet.

Talking with God

Talking with God *is like talking to a friend.* We can talk to Him at any time and any place, 24/7.

We talk to God in our prayers, which are our conversations alone with Him. *God talks to us* through the Bible. When we read and ponder the Holy Word of God, we can hear His voice or sense His "nudging." That nudging is the prompting of His Spirit.

Talking with God *is believing that He truly listens to us.*

Psalm 66:16 tells us that God listens and hears our voice when our hearts are sincere and pure.

Talking with God *is believing that He truly cares about our concerns.*

1 Peter 5:7 says to cast "all your cares, all your anxieties, all your worries, all your concerns, once and for all on Him, for He cares for you affectionately, and cares about you watchfully."[1]

Talking with God *is believing that He can help us if He so desires.*

Psalm 115:3 tells us that our Heavenly Father does whatever pleases Him to do.

Talking with God *is believing that He knows about every minute detail of our lives.*

Matthew 10:30 tells us that the very hairs of our head are not only known by God, but they are all numbered.

Talking with God *is believing that He wants to do His best for those that believe in Him.*

Ephesians 1:5 tells us that God decided in advance to adopt us into His own family by bringing us to Himself through His son Christ Jesus. This is what He wanted to do, and it gave Him great pleasure.

Talking with God *is believing that the Holy Spirit lives within each of us, in His holy Sanctuary, where we can go in secret and we can experience a personal relationship with Him.*

Shall we join Him?

Our bodies have become the temple of God
through the Spirit,
and our hearts his lovely garden.
It is in this garden he dwells;
it is there he walks.

~ See 2 Corinthians 6:16

Section I
Alone with
God
in His Sanctuary

1

Your Sanctuary: The Temple of the Holy Spirit

Do you not know that your body is the temple,
the very Sanctuary of the Holy Spirit
Who lives within you,
whom you have received as a Gift from God?

~ 1 Corinthians 6:19[1]

Have you ever imagined what it would be like to be alone with God in a quiet, peaceful place and have a conversation with Him? What would you talk about? What questions would you ask Him?

The Lord tells us in Jeremiah 29:12-13 that all you have to do is call upon Him and pray to Him and He will listen to you. When you seek Him with all of your heart, you can find Him.

You can personally experience what it's like to be alone with the Living God because He lives in

His Sanctuary—a sacred place of communion with Him within your physical body. It's a secret hiding place where you can be alone with God, where no one else can enter. You can go there any time of the day or night; His Sanctuary is also your sanctuary.

The apostle Paul says that you are the temple of the living God who lives in you and walks with you (2 Corinthians 6:16). Therefore, your temple (where God dwells in you) is your Sanctuary. It's not a beautiful building made by human hands. It's an eternal, sacred place where your soul can be nurtured in perfect harmony with God, where your spiritual life may be protected. It's a place where you can find spiritual rest and peace no matter what difficulties you face each day.

This is true because God loves you; He desires to dwell in you and walk and talk with you, so He has sent His Holy Spirit to live within your Sanctuary 24/7. He's not sitting on a white cloud looking down on you, sending you care packages. He's your personal, living God. Hebrews 13:5 says that He will never leave you nor forsake you. He's with you always. He's a part of you and you're a part of Him. He's closer than breathing and nearer than your own heartbeat.

God is always in your secret place, your Sanctuary within your very being, waiting for you to knock on the door and join Him in reverent communion. He is your Creator, the Architect of the Universe and beyond. He is Holy, love, truth, and a mighty, awesome God. And yet He knows and loves you and me. It's hard to imagine! If it weren't for God's only begotten Son, Christ Jesus, who came to earth to die for us, who shed His blood on the cross at Calvary, and who gifted us His mercy and grace, we would not be worthy to approach His Holy throne room nor be in His presence.

Because we believe that God is our loving Father who wants to have a close, personal relationship with us, then we can envision having conversations with Him. Naturally, you won't actually see God, but you will know that He is with you and you can feel His presence.

WHO IS GOD, THE ONE YOU WILL BE MEETING IN YOUR SANCTUARY?

The Bible says that the Living God is really three persons, a Trinity:

God, the Father;
God, the Son Christ Jesus; and
God, the Holy Spirit.

The moment you receive Christ as your Savior, the Holy Spirit comes to live in your heart, binding His Spirit with your own spirit, bringing you into conformity to His will. Your body becomes the temple of the Holy Spirit, and the Holy Spirit helps you to live the Christian life.

God is both infinite (transcendent) and personal (immanent): he is infinite in that he is not subject to any of the limitations of humanity or of creation in general. He is far greater than everything he has made, far greater than anything else that exists. But he is also personal: he interacts with you as a person, and you can relate to him as a person. You can pray to him, worship him, obey him, and love him, and he can speak to you, rejoice in you, and love you. Apart from the true teachings found in the Bible, no system of religion has a living God who is both infinite and personal.

Don't be confused by these other religious systems. God did not send his Son Christ Jesus to die on the cross for a religion or dogma. Religion today is man-centered, not God-centered. Religion is about rules and regulations; it's about performing activities in the weakness of our strength. A relationship with Christ Jesus, on the other hand, is about trusting in the power of *His* strength to accomplish His will and His plans.

Religion is man's attempt to reach God—Christianity is God's attempt to reach man through His son Christ Jesus. When we understand this, we realize that Christianity is not a religion or religious discipline; it's a relationship. It's about God's desire to reveal Himself to us and our passion to seek, love, and interact with Him.

Having an intimate, personal relationship with God may be difficult for some, especially if your relationship with your earthly father has not been a good experience. Or you may feel that you don't have oneness with God; perhaps there is unconfessed sin keeping you separated from Him; perhaps you don't feel worthy or good enough to talk to God; perhaps your image of God is that He is judgmental and condemning; or perhaps you were never told about our loving, Living God: the Father,

Son, and Holy Spirit who lives in you. He still loves you and desires to commune with you.

WHO IS ABBA FATHER?

"Abba Father" is an endearing expression in the Bible that refers to the Father-child relationship we have with God. Romans 8:15 says that when we ask Christ Jesus into our lives, we become sons and daughters of God, accepted and loved by Him as His children. Therefore, we're supposed to come to God as children coming to our Father, with child-like simplicity of faith. However, His love and tender mercies far exceed that of an earthly parent.

It is in our childlikeness and reverential manner that we can look up to Him and call him Abba Father—Heavenly Daddy. It's a wondrous and comforting experience to be alone with our infinite God and say to Him, "I love you, my Father," with the realization of knowing that you are His beloved child.

Our Awesome, Almighty, Great, and Holy God is also our "Heavenly Daddy," who loves us, holds us, listens to us, and talks to us personally.

WHY ARE WE ABLE TO COMMUNICATE WITH OUR FATHER?

We can call God our Abba Father because, by the Holy Spirit, we are adopted into the Family of God. We can personally communicate with our Heavenly Father because, as believers in the Lord Christ

Jesus, we have the Holy Spirit of God abiding in us. Where His Spirit dwells, there He dwells; and He dwells in our hearts by faith. By our faith we are united and one with Christ and can commune with Him in a very personal way.

Communing with God is reading His Word, the Holy Bible; it's talking to God, thanking Him, praising Him, and worshiping Him. It's confessing our sins to Him, a personal cleansing, through repentance. It's also telling Him the desires of our heart. We do all of this when we come into His presence in our Sanctuary.

To be alone with God in your Sanctuary is the highest joy you can imagine, just as King David said, "The one thing I ask of the Lord–the thing I seek most–is to live in the house of the LORD all the days of my life, delighting in the LORD's perfections and meditating in his Temple (Psalm 27:4)."

I have felt what David felt. And when I neglect spending quiet time with God, my life is out of balance and upside down! When I neglect God, I don't have inner peace and joy that only comes from God. I have been out of balance too many times; I know the difference between living in daily conversation with God and without Him.

Spending time with the Lord is a daily commitment. The more time you spend with Him, the more your life will reflect His character. When you set aside time for the Lord, your concerns are His concerns. He loves you unconditionally and, in knowing that, you can experience the deepest, most wonderful tranquility. After all, He is the Prince of Peace.

Your Pipeline to Father God

We all have a direct "pipeline" to God, His Son, and His Holy Spirit. That pipeline is prayer. When you seek to be in His presence, you can talk to Him. When you pray, you are drawn into a deeper, more intimate relationship with Him.

Christ Jesus says that when you pray, you're to go into your room, your Sanctuary, and when you shut the door, you are to pray to your Father, who is in this secret place. That's when your Father, who sees what you do in secret will reward you openly (see Matthew 6:6). Your Father sees, hears, and knows your needs far more than you know yourself. We'll learn more about prayer in chapter 7.

Can You Really Hear from God?

> Let us labor for an inward stillness and an inward healing— that perfect silence where our heart is still, and we no longer have our own imperfect thoughts and vain opinions. But God alone speaks in us, and we wait in singleness of heart that we may know His will, and in the silence of our spirits, that we may do His will and do that only.
>
> - Henry Wadsworth Longfellow,
> American Poet

If you can hear what God is saying to you, He would tell you things you could not have known on your own. He would give you discernment and wisdom to know right from wrong. You would know His will for your life.

God wants you to know all of this and more, and He tells you how: "Meditate within your heart . . . and be still. Offer the sacrifices of righteousness, and put your trust in the Lord" (Psalm 4:4-5).

What does it mean to meditate, to offer sacrifices, and to trust?

To *meditate is to* ponder, contemplate, and reflect on God's words. Meditating allows you to listen to what the Holy Spirit is nudging you to do.

To *offer sacrifices of righteousness* is to give up what the world desires and, instead, do what is pleasing to God.

To *trust in the Lord is* to confidently hope in and rely on God, that His Word is truth. We'll look at this in more detail in chapter 5.

To do what is pleasing to God and trust in His word requires not only reading His word, but also being still long enough to ponder it and listen to what the Holy Spirit is revealing to you. When I try to be still, reflect on, and listen to what God is saying, my mind tends to wander in two to three directions at the same time. That's the reason I often talk and read aloud during my time alone with God in my Sanctuary, so that I can concentrate on Him and hear His voice and the promptings of His Spirit.

Listen . . .

Do you hear the voice of God?

I have heard His voice only a few times in my life. Most often I don't actually hear that "still small voice" clearly, but I do get nudges about things He wants me to do, sometimes more directly than others. And sometimes I don't want to do what God is prompting me to do, so I say to myself, "Oh, that's not from God," only to realize later that I should have listened more closely. Writing down these nudges in a journal or notebook, as you'll find in Section IV, helps me to remember His promptings and see how they have come to pass in my life. Pages are also provided for you to write down your prayer requests and responses from God in Section III.

When it's difficult to hear God's voice or feel His Spirit nudge you, trust that He wants to communicate with you. Rely on the words that Christ Jesus Himself said:

> Ask and it will be given to you; seek and you will find; knock and the door will be opened to you. For everyone who asks, receives; and he who seeks, finds; and to him who knocks the door will be opened (Mathew 7:7-8).

Take a moment to be still and meditate on this promise. Read it slowly a few times. Ponder it. Reflect on how it relates to your relationship to God at this time in your life.

What is Christ Jesus asking you to do so that you can really hear from God, if not in voice, then in Spirit?

Will you do it?

2

Developing the Ultimate Relationship

And they heard the voice of the LORD walking in the garden.

~ Genesis 3:8

For any relationship to grow and develop, we need to spend time communicating with and loving the other person. God wants a relationship like that with us. He wants to love us and communicate with us, deepening and strengthening our relationship with Him.

The difference in our relationship with the Heavenly Father and an earthly relationship with our family and friends is that we are not our own. We belong to God. We are bought with a price—the blood of Christ Jesus—and we are inhabited by the Holy Spirit (1 Corinthians 6:19-20).

It is within our own Sanctuary that God reveals Himself to us. Pouring Himself into our waiting spirits, He fills us with His love. Our love relationship with God is strengthened every time we reenter our Sanctuary and He talks with us in deepest secrecy. In his book, *Food for the Lambs,*[1] Charles Ebert Orr explains it this way:

> What an honor it is to have an audience with the King of glory! He extends the golden scepter to us, and we come hopefully, confidently, into His presence and tell Him all that is in our hearts. It is only because we comprehend something of His great love to us that we venture to come into His presence. The greatest honor bestowed upon man is the privilege of coming into the presence of God and conversing with Him.

In our Sanctuary, we come into the presence of God who, the Bible tells us, knows us intimately. He knew us before the foundation of the world. He knows the number of days He has allotted to each of us on this earth. And He knows the number of hairs on our head.

God wants us to know Him intimately as He knows us. He does not hide His heart from us. In Jeremiah 24:7, God says, "I will give them a heart to know me." The way to know God's heart is to read His Holy Word, accepting His Son Christ Jesus into our lives, and having the Holy Spirit live in us. Once God takes up residence in us, He wants us to spend time with Him.

Can you envision walking with Christ Jesus on a narrow pathway in a beautiful garden? He holds your hand as you walk, talking about the cares of your day. Even laughing! Although you want Him to hold your hand tight and never let go, He also allows you to pull away from Him, running off to see what you can explore. He gives you this free will, even though it might get you into trouble.

As you return to the Lord's path and reach for His hand, consider singing this hymn to your loving Father:

Precious Lord, take my hand, help me stand.
I am tired, I am weak, I am worn.
Through the storm, through the night
lead me on to the light,
Take my hand precious Lord,
lead me home.[2]

As you take His hand and reenter your Sanctuary, the secret place of the most high, your focus will be on God, through Christ Jesus. There, you can be empowered by the Holy Spirit to know His will and do His will.

As we've seen, the enemy of our soul wants to destroy and conquer this kind of intimacy with our Father in Heaven. I keep this in mind so that when I'm having a busy workday, I consciously take just a few minutes to slow down and reenter my Sanctuary to "rest in the Lord and wait patiently for Him" as Psalm 37:7 says.[3] To truly rest in the Lord, I come to Him with a child-like faith and trust, asking the Lord to lead me into His perfect will for my life.

Can you imagine how much better you would feel if you took a few precious minutes out of your busy day to retreat into your Sanctuary and not only talk to God as your Abba Father, but praise and love God for all He has done for you? Yes, to delight in and express the magnificence of God helps us nurture intimacy with Him as well.

You can praise, worship, and delight in the Lord in whatever way you choose: perhaps singing songs of inspiration and thanksgiving, writing a poem of glory to God, painting a landscape of Him where He dwells. Can you imagine that God might have a smile on his face when you do that?

In the midst of all the problems that overwhelm life, it's comforting to know that you can seek God in your quiet, secret Sanctuary within you at any time—a holy place of praising and resting in the arms of your Almighty God.

David shares with us in Psalm 91 his intimate relationship with God who shelters him within his Sanctuary:

Those who live in the shelter of the Most High
  will find rest in the shadow of the Almighty.

This I declare about the Lord:
  He alone is your refuge, your place of safety;
  He is your God, and you can trust him.

For He will rescue you from every trap
  and protect you from deadly disease.

He will cover you with his feathers.
  He will shelter you with his wings.

His faithful promises are your armor and protection.
Do not be afraid of the terrors of the night,
nor the arrow that flies in the day.
Do not dread the disease that stalks in darkness,
nor the disaster that strikes at midday.
Though a thousand fall at your side,
though ten thousand are dying around you,
these evils will not touch you.
Just open your eyes, and see how the wicked
are punished.
If you make the LORD your refuge,
if you make the Most High your shelter,
no evil will conquer you;
no plague will come near your home.
For He will order His angels
to protect you wherever you go.
They will hold you up with their hands
so you won't even hurt your foot on a stone.
You will trample upon lions and cobras;
you will crush fierce lions and serpents under
your feet!
The LORD says, "I will rescue those who love me.
I will protect those who trust in my name.
"When they call on me, I will answer;
I will be with them in trouble.
I will rescue and honor them.
"I will reward them with a long life
and give them my salvation.[4]

When you develop a personal, intimate relationship with the Heavenly Father, you will abide under the shadow of the Almighty who supplies all your needs and restores your soul. He is within you always, living in your Sanctuary, and will never give up on you.

The words of Dottie Rambo's Southern Gospel song tell of God's presence within us: "So let the storm clouds rage and the dark clouds rise, they don't bother me; for I'm sheltered in the arms of God. He walks with me, and nothing on earth shall harm me, for I'm sheltered in the arms of God."

God loves you unconditionally. He also wants the very best for your life. You simply need to love Him, trust Him, and believe with assurance that you are never alone. He holds your hand and walks with you through all the trials you face.

Charles Ebert Orr gives us a clear insight into the importance of our being alone with God:

> Our lives will never be all they should be unless we are much alone with God. When amid the active duties of life, we can scarcely come into that sacred nearness to God that will enable us to feel in our hearts all that God is. We may get slight glimpses of His glory, we may occasionally get a dim view of some of His beauty, we may feel a little warming of His love in our bosoms; but only when alone with Him are we awed into wonder at the sight of His glory and great beauty. It is only then that our hearts can be deeply impressed with the knowledge that He is God, and in childlikeness we can look up to Him and call Him Abba Father.[5]

Once you enter your sanctuary, what exactly do you do there? The next section will explain how I use the Bible, prayer, and a journal (found later in this book) to deepen my relationship with my Father.

3

Keep the Enemy out of Your Sanctuary

Although I grew up in a Christian-believing home, I have neglected my relationship with God more than I have sought Him. This was especially true during the many years I was involved in the occult.

When I was young, my parents were ministers of music and members of a Southern Gospel quartet that sang in churches of all Christian denominations throughout the Midwest. As an only child, I traveled and often sang with them. I heard the spoken Word hundreds of times before the age of ten.

When I entered college, I turned my back on my Christian up-bringing. I sought out other religions, eager to try all the things the world had to offer. My curiosity led me to explore astrology, numerology, aura enlightenment, reincarnation, karma, and Transcendental Meditation.

For seven years, I also studied the works of Rudolph Steiner who founded the Anthroposophical Society, which believes that man has all the wisdom within himself to solve the riddles of existence. God is not needed.

During my initiation ceremony into Transcendental Meditation, I was given my special word—a "mantra" chosen "just for me" by the initiators. I had to repeat it in silence over and over for twenty minutes in the morning and twenty minutes in the evening. This was supposed to help me to "transcend" into a relaxed state of consciousness. It worked. I did!

However, after I had become depressed and suicidal several months later, I found out that the mantra I had been given was actually the name of a Hindu god. Just imagine . . . by repeating the word over and over, I was praying to and worshiping one of the many Hindu gods! The Bible refers to these practices as an abomination to the Lord. The Lord our God said in His Ten Commandments that we should have no other gods before Him.

I had to get to a state of deep depression in order to cry out for help to the Living God, not some impersonal "force" or "energy" or "inner wisdom." I finally realized what the apostle Paul knew when he wrote Ephesians 6:10-12: that my struggle with depression was not against flesh and blood, but against the rulers, against the authorities, against the powers of this dark world, and against the spiritual forces of evil in the heavenly realms.

In spite of my many sins, my Heavenly Father showed me that I was extremely valuable to Him because He sent His son Christ Jesus to die for me, erasing all my sins. I thank God that I was delivered from that spiritual bondage.

The words of the hymn "It Is Well with My Soul" say it clearly:

My sins, not in part but the whole,
are nailed to the cross,
and I bear them no more.
Praise the Lord, praise the Lord, O my Soul![1]

Even though I had been set free from the occult, I still found it difficult to consistently walk with the Lord. I refer to those times as being in a "desert place" where my soul was wandering through a barren wasteland, thirsting for happiness but not finding relief.

I have been in that dry and desolate desert place many times throughout my life. I tried to have a close, personal relationship with God, but not by reading His word, so I still felt empty. It was as if He was withholding His presence from me so that I would seek Him, pursue Him, and thirst for Him even more.

Psalm 42:1-2 says,

> As the deer pants for streams of water, so my soul yearns for Him. My soul thirsts for God, the Living God. When can I meet with God?

That is what I asked myself, *when?* When can I meet with you, God?

I didn't know yet that our God is a jealous God. Just as he wanted to spend time with me, I had to get to the point that I yearned for Him.

David understood this when he said in Psalm 63:1-5:

> O God, you are my God, earnestly I seek you; my soul thirsts for you, my body longs for you, in a dry and weary land where there is no water. I have seen you in the sanctuary and beheld your power and your glory. Because your love is better than life, my lips will glorify you. I will praise you as long as I live, and in your name I will lift up my hands. My soul will be satisfied as with the richest of foods; with singing lips my mouth will praise you.

In my deep thirst for God, I set aside time to spend with Him and study His Word. Only then did I begin to feel the presence of God, hold his hand, and feel His nudges.

I have to admit that there are still times in my life when I choose to let go of God's hand, walk away from His presence, and enter the desert place once more. Sometimes several months pass before I reach out for God again. But He is always faithful to forgive me, take my hand, and hold it tight . . . *until I choose to let go again.*

Although God is consistent and faithful with us, living a consistent life as a Christian believer is not easy. It's far easier to follow the enticements of the world, but God designed the well of our souls. He will keep us reaching for Him so that He can fill our well and renew us with His living water.

> Those who drink the water I give them will never be thirsty again. It becomes a fresh, bubbling spring within them, giving eternal life (John 4:14 NLT).

Have you been in a "desert place" or are you in it now?

Can you describe how it feels to be in that desert place?

Have you ever spent time reading God's word and meditating on it?

What difference in your life have you experienced when you read and meditate on God's word?

Our Enemy Keeps Us Distracted

I am ashamed that I spent so much time living in the sins of the world and the occult when I could have been sitting at the feet of Christ Jesus, listening to His teachings. I'm no longer distracted by the occult, but I am distracted by my busy life, career, and caring for my family. Sometimes, I'm just too tired to talk to God or seek Him, so I fall asleep instead. Even today, it's still easier to pursue my own desires than take the time to develop a true relationship with God. These distractions put me back in that desert place where I feel so alone, because I'm not being nurtured and fed spiritually.

Satan knows that you, too, need the serene times of fellowship with the Lord so that you can be lifted out of your daily grind of existence, so he keeps you distracted. If he cannot have your soul, then he loves stealing your time with activities that seem important. Satan is the great deceiver and liar who loves that we love our own desires, and he helps us to pursue them - even in ways that seem Christian-like. Just think of how much time you might make for family, friends, work, parties, television, sports, and entertainment but little time for a quiet moment alone with God.

The enemy of your soul will keep you so distracted from entering your Sanctuary that you won't even be able to find the path that leads to it. Yet God is always wooing you to Himself, no matter how much you get distracted or how far you stray from Him. Even if you can't hear Him or see Him, God wants you to pursue Him.

Frederick W. Faber, a British rector, once said, "There is hardly ever a complete silence in our soul. God is whispering to us incessantly. Whenever the sounds of the world die out in the soul, or sink low, then we hear these whisperings of God. He is always whispering to us, only we do not always hear because of the hurry, noise, and distraction which life causes as it rushes on."[2]

Where Are You, God?

Each day we face obstacles that complicate our lives and test our faith: fear, depression, illness, financial hardship, oppression, defeat, negativity, lack of faith, worry, failure, panic attacks, anxiety, discouragement. We cry out, where are you, God? When we feel helpless or hopeless in the situation, we are comforted knowing that when we close our eyes and visualize reentering our peaceful Sanctuary within each of us, we can rest in the arms of God and tell our Abba Father about our problems, believing that He will deliver us from them. God is always with us, within us.

Is your life full of busyness? Do you feel as though your life is out of control? Are you stressed out? Have you been in a dry and desolate "desert place" seeking the source of the living water but finding none? Do you feel as though you're running down a myriad of paths, but not the path to your Sanctuary where your Father God waits? Is something blocking your path? If you answered yes to any of these, you need to reroute your soul into the place of refuge where you can enjoy the warmth of God's presence and the confidence of feeling His hand in yours.

The place of refuge is in His holy Sanctuary.

God loves you and desires to live within you.

Will you join Him?

4

Prepare to Enter His Sanctuary

Our Sanctuary within us is a resting place for
our soul where we can find quiet in the love of
God just as Christ Jesus asks us to do:
"Come to Me, all you who labor and are heavy-
laden and over burdened,
and I will cause you to rest.
I will ease and relieve and refresh your souls."

~ Matthew 11:28 NASB

Our inner Sanctuary is not to be confused with any New Age ideas of becoming one with a universal force. It's not to be confused with Eastern or mystical meditation, which incorrectly assumes that the answers to life lie within ourselves. It's about meeting the personal God who created the universe and His Holy Spirit where they naturally dwell–within us.

We are not sufficient enough to think that anything we do or accomplish came wholly from ourselves, but all our sufficiency is of God; we owe Him all the praise and glory of the good that is done, and from Him we must receive grace and strength to do more. That's what 2 Corinthians 3:4-5 says. If we are to accomplish anything for God, we must personally meet with God who dwells in us.

Does God *really* dwell in us?

Yes, and we are assured of this by the apostles who spoke about it: "If anyone acknowledges that Jesus is the Son of God, God lives in him and he in God," said the apostle John in 1 John 4:16 (NIV). And the apostle Paul asked the Corinthians, "Do you know that you are the temple and God's Spirit lives in you?" (1 Corinthians 3:16).[1]

If we truly believe that God's Holy Spirit lives within our physical bodies, wouldn't we want to keep our bodies healthy and pure as we were told in 1 Corinthians 6:19-20:

> Don't you realize that your body is the temple of the Holy Spirit, who lives in you and was given to you by God? You do not belong to yourself, for God bought you with a high price. So you must honor God with your body.

It's hard to comprehend where God dwells in us; it's a highly spiritual location that we won't fully fathom until we become one with Christ Jesus forever. While we journey toward that eternal time and place, we can make his dwelling in us more accessible by imagining it as a real Sanctuary where Christ Jesus waits for us.

Meeting Him in this way will help us to feel God's presence and love on a deeper, personal level. Of course, imagining an actual Sanctuary is not necessary for developing a relationship with God, but it has helped me to feel a closer connection with my Father in Heaven, and I believe it will for you, too.

Before I guide you into your own Sanctuary, let me describe how I enter mine.

Preparing to Enter My Sanctuary

In preparation for spending time alone with God in my Sanctuary, my secret place of the most high, I find a place where I have no distractions and can sit comfortably. I close my eyes to focus on becoming quiet, trying to calm my fleeting thoughts so that I can concentrate on my relationship with my Almighty God. To know God requires that I be still and seek solitude with my loving Father who tells us,

> Be still, and know that I am God! (Psalm 46:10).

Be still? I have a difficult time trying to be still; I'm constantly in the process of learning to do that! So I sit relatively still, close my eyes, and envision that my holy Sanctuary is a room within my body, located near my heart. To get to that room, I picture myself walking along a pathway in a beautiful spring garden decorated with a palette of wild flowers. Their fragrance fills every breath. The birds sing God's praises as they soar along in the blue heavens. Small animals run about, especially little dogs! I soon approach an ivy-framed doorway. A tinge of excitement pulsates in my heart knowing that my Heavenly Father is waiting for me to reenter our Sanctuary.

I gently knock on the door where my Abba Father dwells. He opens it and says, "Come in, my child, I've been waiting for you."

I enter a tiny one-room log cabin. Redwood planks cover the floor and rough log paneling line the walls. To my right stands a simple wooden table with a matching chair behind it. To my left sits a grandfather-sized rocking chair facing a fully bloomed Star Magnolia tree outside the open window.

The room is illuminated with the light from God's presence. He stands with outstretched arms. I walk toward Him. He gives me a big hug and says, "My child, I've missed you." He picks me up and carries me to that welcoming rocking chair where He puts me in His lap, wraps me in His loving arms, and holds me while we rock back and forth. I can feel His purity and the warmth of His love.

"My child, tell me what's happening in your life and what I can do to help today?" He says.

I hesitate, wondering how much I should share. Then I recall 1 Peter 5:7, which says to cast all my cares, all my anxieties, all my worries, all my concerns, once and for all on Him; for He cares for me affectionately and cares about me watchfully.

Believing that He truly knows, loves, and cares about me personally and all of my many problems allows me to relax, rest in His arms, and tell Him everything.

Why not cast all your worries and concerns upon the Lord? He cares about you and He wants to bear all your burdens. Why not let Him?

Preparing to Enter Your Sanctuary

How do you envision your Sanctuary, where the Father , Son, and Holy Spirit dwell? What do you see? What do you hear? What do you smell?

Your inner Sanctuary could be elaborate or simple. Perhaps you envision a gazebo with two white wicker chairs in the middle of a garden with lovely, colorful, fragrant flowers. Or it might be a meadow with a flowing stream running through it and a soft quilt to lie upon and rest in God's presence as warm breezes caress your face.

You might envision your Sanctuary as sitting on a large rock overlooking the majestic ocean with white, fluffy clouds hovering high in the blue sky as you talk with God.

Or you may simply envision holding God's hand as you walk along the pathway in a forest of tall trees, talking, laughing, and sharing your innermost feelings.

The words to the song "In the Garden" come to mind:

I come to the garden alone,
while the dew is still on the roses;
and the voice I hear, falling on my ear,
the Son of God discloses.

He speaks, and the sound of His voice
is so sweet the birds hush their singing.
And the melody that He gave to me
within my heart is ringing.

I'd stay in the garden with Him
though the night around me be falling.
But He bids me go through the voice of woe,
His voice to me is calling.

And He walks with me, and He talks with me,
and He tells me I am His own;
and the joy we share as we tarry there,
none other has ever known.[2]

Be still. Do you hear His voice calling you so softly and tenderly? Know that your Heavenly Father wants you to come to Him. Know that God's perfect Sanctuary is within you, where He dwells. Know that He is waiting for you to come to Him when you need His healing touch.

Be still. He's calling your name. He loves you and longs to talk with you. He wants you to praise and worship Him.

Be still and know that He is God.

Whatever peaceful place you envision, it's your own secret Sanctuary, a holy place of resting in the arms of your Abba Father, your Heavenly Daddy, where you can build an intimate relationship with Him.

Section II

Affirmations of the Christian Faith

5

Meditate on Affirmations of the Christian Faith

Several years ago, in my quest to draw closer to God, I began compiling in a journal Scriptures of the Holy Bible that I believed to be the foundation of my core beliefs as a Christian, a declaration of my faith. Over the years, I continued to add more verses in my journal. As I read them aloud to God in my devotion time alone with Him in my quiet Sanctuary within, it became evident I was making affirmations of the Christian faith in the form of prayer—prayer grounded in the word of God.

"Praying" these Scriptures has given meaning and clarity to the Christian doctrine in a very personal way. As a result, my faith and relationship with my Abba Father have grown and strengthened.

These affirmations of faith are written in the first person as paraphrases of Scripture. They are personal, positive declarations of worship, praise, and thanksgiving to God. Personalizing the Scriptures with "I" and reading them aloud with reverence is one way I talk directly to God.

The words of the Scriptures move from my lips to my mind, and then into my heart, making each passage my own.

Each Scripture is intended for my spiritual strengthening. But it's also like reading a love letter to God. They are words to worship Him, thank Him, and praise Him for who He is and for all that He does in my life. They are words of inspiration when I am in doubt. They are words of encouragement when I need to be lifted up. They are words of comfort when I feel alone.

These words also keep my knowledge of Christian teaching in perspective as to who God is; He is a Living God that you and I can experience through a personal relationship with Christ Jesus. These words give me comfort as I focus on how much He loves me and all that He does for me every second of every day.

Some days I read all the affirmations at one time, in thoughtful meditation. Some days I need to spend more time reflecting on just one passage that speaks to me when I need to hear it most because of what's going on in my life that day.

How I Worship God through Affirmations of Faith

When I read each affirmation, I focus on key words within each passage. For example, I have bolded these words in the first few affirmations. I think about the meaning of each word and how it relates to me. Under each selection is the Scripture the affirmation is based on.

Let's take a meditative walk through my Sanctuary as we look at the first affirmation:

Thank you, Heavenly Father,
for Your ever-present Sanctuary within me—
my "Secret Place of the Most High,"
where I can rest in Your presence.
You are my **refuge**, my **fortress**,
and my Almighty God in whom I trust.

(Psalm 91:1-2)

After reading this slowly, I might reflect on the word **refuge** and think that God is a lighthouse in the storms of life that surround me. He shines His beacon of light in the darkness to guide and direct my pathway. This reminds me of Psalm 119:105, which says, "Your word is a lamp to my feet and a light for my path." For a moment, I ponder and reflect on this verse, perhaps concentrating on the word **light** or **path.** I ask God to help me stay on the lighted path that leads to Him.

The word **fortress** reminds me that God shelters me. He's my protector, keeping me safe from harm. I remind myself of the times that God has kept me safe, and I praise Him for being my refuge and my fortress.

I move on to the second affirmation:

I approach Your **Holy** throne of grace
with **reverence** and adoration,
with the assurance that I may receive
your mercy and grace
(Hebrews 4:16)

After reading this passage, I sometimes focus on the meaning of the word **Holy** and think of God's holiness and purity. He is to be honored and revered, worshiped and praised, loved and adored.

It is in this passage that I feel unworthy to enter into His Holy throne of grace. But He tells us that we are to come to Him with **reverence** and a godly fear, invited to the mercy seat where God reigns. He tells us to come to His throne of Grace to receive **mercy,** to pardon our sins, and receive **grace** to purify our souls.

When I read this next Scripture, I often dwell on the words **Abba Father**.

I experience the blessing of knowing
that You, my **Abba Father,**
hear and answer my prayers
because I strive to obey Your commands
and to do what pleases You.
(1 John 3:22)

I truly love the vision of my Heavenly Daddy holding me in His loving arms as we rock back and forth in His big rocking chair. I always grin from ear to ear when I think of that. If I were an artist, I'd transfer that image onto canvas. I take comfort in knowing that my Father listens to my problems and answers my prayers when they are for my highest good.

In the next affirmation, I spend time on the words **heart, soul, mind**, and **strength**.

I love You, Heavenly Father,
with all my **heart**,
I love You with all my **soul**,
I love You with all my **mind**,
And I love You with all my **strength**.

(Mark 12:30)

I say, for example, "I love you, Heavenly Father, with all the **love** that I have in every fiber of my being." Or, "I love you, Heavenly Father, with all my **mind**, with all of my knowledge of knowing who you are.

Sometimes I also meditate on the Scripture that the affirmation is based on. This often brings further inspiration and more opportunities to ponder and reflect on God's truth. These Scriptures are noted under each affirmation.

Who Can Read These Affirmations?

These affirmations of the Christian faith are intended for those who know Christ Jesus and believe in His truths. Practicing a religion without a personal encounter with Christ Jesus does not save your soul. The cross where Christ Jesus gave His life for you is the only place you can find forgiveness and eternal life with God the Father.

If you have not accepted Christ Jesus as your personal savior and you want to have an intimate relationship with Him, you may do so at any time by saying the following prayer:

Heavenly Father, I come to You in prayer,
asking You to forgive my sins.
I confess with my mouth
and believe with my heart
that Christ Jesus is Your only begotten son,
that He was crucified on the cross and died for me,
and that His shed blood cleansed me of all my sins.
I believe that Christ Jesus rose from the dead
and ascended into Heaven.
I ask You to come into my life
and be my personal Lord and Savior.
I surrender my life to You and
I will worship You all the days of my life
because I believe your Word is truth.
In Jesus' name,
Amen.

Confess That Jesus is Lord

After you have prayed this prayer, it's important to tell someone that you've invited Christ Jesus into your heart. Why? Because "if you confess with your mouth 'Jesus is Lord' and believe in your heart that God raised Him from the dead, you will be saved. For it is with your heart that you believe and are justified, and it is with your mouth that you confess and are saved" (Romans 10:9-10 NIV).

To be saved means that you will live in eternity with your Abba Father, your Heavenly Daddy. Christ Jesus said there is only one door that leads into eternity: "I am the way, the truth and the life. No one comes to the Father except through me" (John 14:6). Jesus is the only way to the Father. Believe it in your heart and confess it with your mouth through these prayers and affirmations.

Confess Your Sins

In addition to confessing publicly that Jesus is Lord, there is a place in the affirmations where you can confess your sins privately to God, asking Him to forgive you. Romans 3:23 says that everyone has sinned and missed the mark of God's perfection. We all continue to fall short of the glory of God.

God sees even the smallest "white lie" as the biggest sin you can possibly imagine. In God's eyes, all sins are created equal. And any sin separates us from God. Your road of life may be paved with good works and good deeds, but those good works and good deeds do not lead you to God. It is such a relief and comfort to know that your wondrous God is so merciful when you ask His forgiveness. It's that simple!

Now that you have asked Christ Jesus to be Lord of your life, you will want to make a public statement of your faith. Baptism is a symbol of death to your old way of life and the new beginning in Christ Jesus. However, it's not a requirement for salvation.

Romans 6:4 succinctly explains why we get baptized: "We have been buried with Him through baptism into death, so that as Christ was raised from the dead through the glory of the Father, so we too might walk in newness of life."

Repent of Your Sins

Now that you have acknowledged that Christ Jesus is your Lord and Savior and have asked Him to forgive your sins, it's time to turn away from those sins and head toward Jesus. It's not always easy to live a life separate from the desires of the world—from your sins. But if you ask Jesus to help you, He will lead you toward Him because He is your Father who always has your best intentions in His will.

Get Ready to Enter

Your time alone in your Sanctuary with your Heavenly Father is a profoundly personal and spiritual experience. It might be difficult at first to concentrate, but as you sit quietly and begin to meditate on the affirmations every day, you will be disciplining your mind to enter your Sanctuary more often with less preparation and at any time of the day.

In your Sanctuary, before you meditate and worship the Lord, you might find it helpful to focus your thoughts onto God's thoughts by applying the passage in Psalm 4 below along with the guiding questions. As you grow in your relationship and intimacy with the Lord, you might find another Scripture to help you focus. You might also write your own guiding questions in your journal. For now, you may start here:

> I will **meditate** within my heart upon my bed (or in my Sanctuary) and be still. I offer you, Father God, the **sacrifices of righteousness**, and put my **trust in the Lord** (Psalm 4:4-5).

Meditate

Take a minute to ponder this affirmation: reflect on one word or phrase for a few minutes. Write the word or phrase in your journal.

Then ask yourself:

1. *What is the Holy Spirit nudging me to think about as I contemplate each word or phrase?*

Write the answer in your journal as well.

Here is an example:

The Holy Spirit has been nudging me to consider my independent nature.

Offer sacrifices of righteousness

Give up worldly desires and do what God desires.

Ask yourself these questions and write the answers in your journal. Examples are provided.

2. *What is God asking me to give up?*

   God is asking me to give up self-reliance.

3. *What is God asking me to do?*

   God is asking me to surround myself with His love and protection.

Trust in the Lord

Rely on these Words as Truth from God Himself. Then ask yourself:

4. *How does God's truth differ from how I have been living?*

   God says that He is my fortress, but I often build my own walls around my heart. The walls are so high, they even keep God out.

Writing your thoughts and feelings in a personal journal as you meditate on His Word are ways to offer praise, giving thanks to God for His majesty and magnificence. There is space for you to write these thoughts starting in Section IV.

6

Enter His Sanctuary

God now invites you to join Him in His holy Sanctuary so that you may receive his grace and peace in the fullest measure, through the knowledge of God and Christ Jesus your Lord (2 Peter 1:2).

The following Scriptures of the Holy Bible are words of worship, praise, and thanksgiving. They are affirmations of faith that keep the Christian doctrine in perspective as to who God is, a Living God, through your personal relationship with Christ Jesus.

All you have to do is envision entering your sacred Sanctuary and experience God's presence as He holds you, enveloping you in His loving arms as He rocks you in His big rocking chair. In your childlikeness you look up to Him, reading the affirmations to Him, confirming your love to Him, dedicating your life to Him, seeking His will, and calling him Abba Father.

I encourage you to develop your intimate relationship with God and worship of Him by meditating on the following Affirmations of the Christian Faith while alone in your Sanctuary with Him as you learned to do in the last chapter. As you do, you will feel the presence of your loving, living, Holy God, and you will be blessed!

Sanctuary Affirmations

Thank you, Heavenly Father,
for Your ever-present Sanctuary within me . . .
my "Secret Place of the Most High,"
where I can rest in Your presence.
You are my refuge, my fortress,
and my Almighty God, in whom I trust.

(Psalm 91:1-2)

I approach Your Holy throne of grace
with reverence and adoration,
with the assurance that I may receive
Your mercy and grace.

(Hebrews 4:16)

I experience the blessing of knowing
that You, my Abba Father,
hear and answer my prayers
because I strive to obey Your commands
and to do what pleases You.

(1 John 3:22)

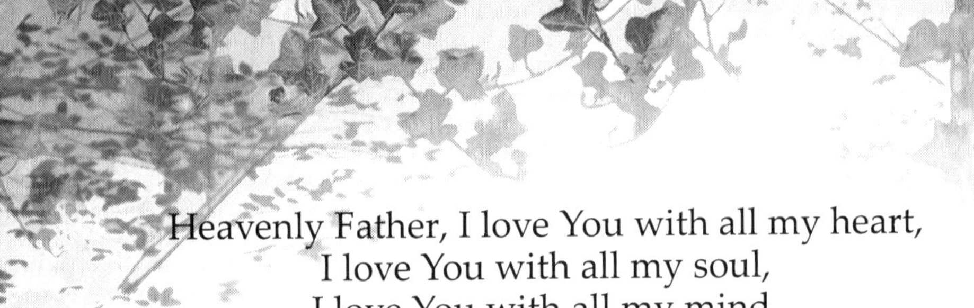

Heavenly Father, I love You with all my heart,
I love You with all my soul,
I love You with all my mind,
and I love You with all my strength.

(Mark 12:30)

You are my almighty God.
By the power of Your spoken word
You willed everything into existence.
You are everything
that ever was, is, and ever shall be.
Your awesome magnitude
is beyond my comprehension,
and I know for certain
that I'm in Your loving care.

(Genesis 1; John 1:1-5; Colossians 1:15-17)

Heavenly Father, thank You for choosing me
before the foundation of the world
and for creating me in your spirit image,
that I should be holy
and blameless in Your sight.

(Ephesians 1:4)

Thank You for loving me so much
that You sent Your Son Christ Jesus to earth
so that I might know His Divine Glory
and choose to believe in Him.

(John 3:16)

Through Your shed blood
on the cross at Calvary,
I have redemption
and Your forgiveness of my sins,
according to the riches of Your grace.

(Ephesians 1:7)

When I confess my sins,
I know You are faithful
and just to forgive my sins
and to cleanse me from all unrighteousness.

(1 John 1:9)

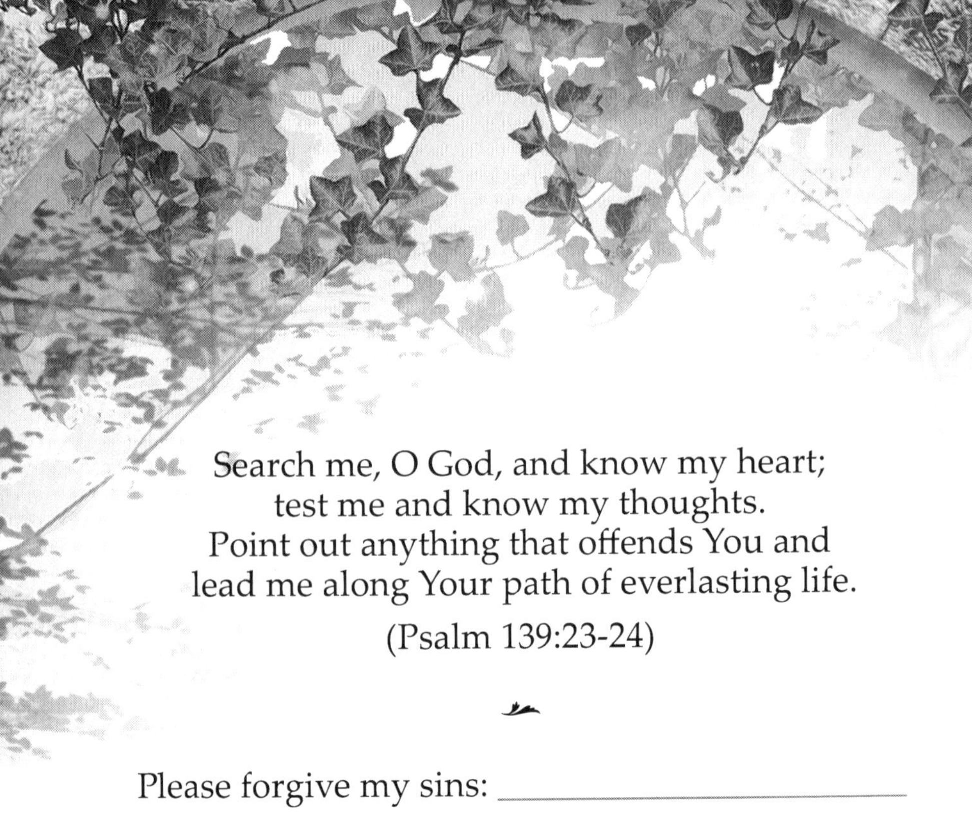

Search me, O God, and know my heart;
test me and know my thoughts.
Point out anything that offends You and
lead me along Your path of everlasting life.

(Psalm 139:23-24)

Please forgive my sins: ______________________________
____
____
____

(Ask God to forgive all of your sins)

Heavenly Father,
I forgive those who have hurt me.
I release all feelings of hurt and anger,
bitterness and resentment.
Help me to know true forgiveness
and to see others as part of You.

(Matthew 6:14-15;
Colossians 3:13-14; Ephesians 4:31-32)

Abba Father,
I'm Your child.
I have inherited Your kingdom, and
I will spend eternity with you
because I've accepted Your Son Christ Jesus
as my Yeshua and Messiah, my personal Savior,
my Redeemer, Master and Lord.

(Matthew 25:34; John 5:24;
Ephesians 1:5-6; Romans 8:15-17)

Thank you for Your Holy Spirit
who dwells within me
because I have been justified
through faith in Christ Jesus
and His atoning death on my behalf.

(Romans 5:1-2; Romans 8:11; Ephesians 1:13-14)

Because the Holy Spirit lives within me,
through my faith in Christ Jesus,
and because I'm trusting in Your promises,
I am able to overcome temptations,
false teachings, and conflicting influences.
I submit to the Holy Spirit's leading
and constantly draw on His power.

(Matthew 7:15, 24:24;
1 John 5:4-5; Ephesians 5:18)

Your Holy Spirit instructs me
in all spiritual things
as I read and constantly meditate
on Your inspired written Word, the Holy Bible,
and as I abide in Christ Jesus.
Thank you, Father God,
for Your living truth
as you speak to me through Your Word.

(John 14:26, 15:7)

I am sanctified by Your Holy Spirit
who works within me
and conforms me into Your image.
You have set me apart
so that I may be complete,
thoroughly equipped,
and prepared for every good work.

(2 Timothy 3:16-17)

My body is the temple of the Holy Spirit,
and so I glorify You, Father God,
with my body and in my spirit.
Teach me to be a responsible steward
of my body,
keeping it healthy and pure.

(1 Corinthians 6:19)

My passion is to know You intimately.
My fervent desire is to love You more deeply
with every fiber of my being.
Thank you for Your sacred presence within me
as I seek Your guidance in everything I do.

(2 Chronicles 7:14-15)

In Your infinite love
You predestined me to do Your will.
I exist for Your glory.
I'm significant because of You.
I pray that Your perfect purpose
be accomplished with the work of Your Spirit
in my heart and life.

(Ephesians 1:11-12)

I submit to Your dominion, power,
and authority over my life,
and I abide in Your will.
Take charge of my life,
and show me Your way,
Heavenly Father,
for I'm ready to receive Your guidance.
I surrender myself completely to You.
Everything I have belongs to You.
I give You my life; I give You my will,
for it is not my will, but Your will be done
on earth as it is in Heaven.
Take my will and use it for Your glory.

(Matthew 6:10)

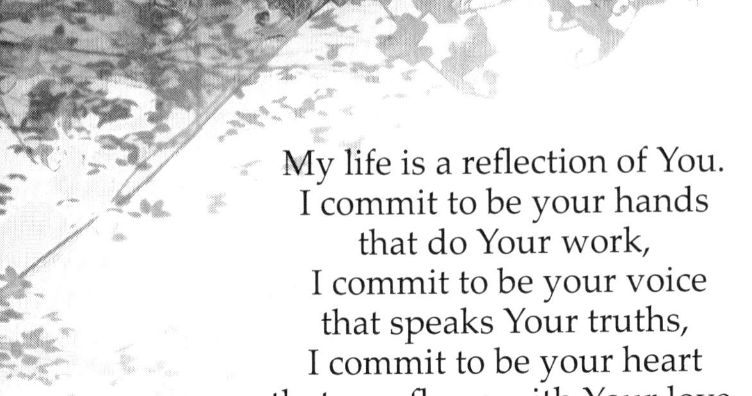

My life is a reflection of You.
I commit to be your hands
that do Your work,
I commit to be your voice
that speaks Your truths,
I commit to be your heart
that overflows with Your love.

(Matthew 9:38)

I joyfully give myself to You
as a living sacrifice for Your service.
I am not conformed to this world,
because You have transformed me
by renewing my mind,
so that I may live to honor and obey You
and to discover what is good and acceptable
in Your perfect will.

(Romans 12:1-2)

Fill me with the knowledge of Your will
in all wisdom and spiritual truths,
that I may be worthy of You, fully pleasing You,
and being fruitful in every good work.

(Colossians 1:9-10)

I worship You, Abba Father, for who You are.
I praise You for what You do in my life.
Help me, O Lord,
to keep Your Ten Commandments
in my heart and mind –
to trust only You,
to worship only You,
to use your name in ways that honor You,
to rest on the Sabbath day
and meditate on You,
to respect and obey my parents,
to protect and respect human life,
to be true to my spouse,
to not take what belongs to others,
to not lie, and
to be satisfied with what I have.

(Exodus 20:1-17)

Father God, help me to live in harmony
with my fellow man,
sympathetic, brotherly, kindhearted,
and humble in spirit;
not returning evil for evil or insult for insult,
but giving a blessing instead.

(1 Peter 3:8-9)

Let love be my top priority in everything I do.
Help me to love others
as You have loved me.

(John 13:34)

Thank you for showing me
Your definition of love:
Love is patient.
Love is kind.
Love is not jealous.
Love does not brag
and is not arrogant.
Love does not act unbecomingly
and does not seek its own.
Love is not easily angered
and does not keep a record of wrongs.
Love does not delight in evil,
but rejoices with the truth.
Love always protects,
always trusts,
always hopes,
and love always perseveres.
Love never fails!

(1 Corinthians 13:4-7)

Let my love radiate to all people
and be an inspiration to help lift others.
Help me to remember that it's not about me,
it's about You, Father God.

Holy Spirit, fill me
with Your fruit of the Spirit,
so that I may exhibit the Christ-like
characteristics of
His Love,
His Joy,
His Peace,
His Patience,
His Kindness,
His Goodness,
His Faithfulness,
His Gentleness,
His Self Control.

(Galatians 5:22-23)

I dedicate my life to You, Heavenly Father,
as Your obedient servant
in faithful and joyful service.
I choose to serve You, Father God.
Show me how I can serve You today,
and I will obey You.

(Psalm 119:33-36)

Thank You, Abba Father,
for imparting Your spiritual gifts to me
so that I may use them to glorify You
and to help those who believe in You.

(Romans 12:6-8)

I shall serve You, Father God,
with the talents and abilities
that You have given me
to meet the needs of others.

(Matthew 25:34-46)

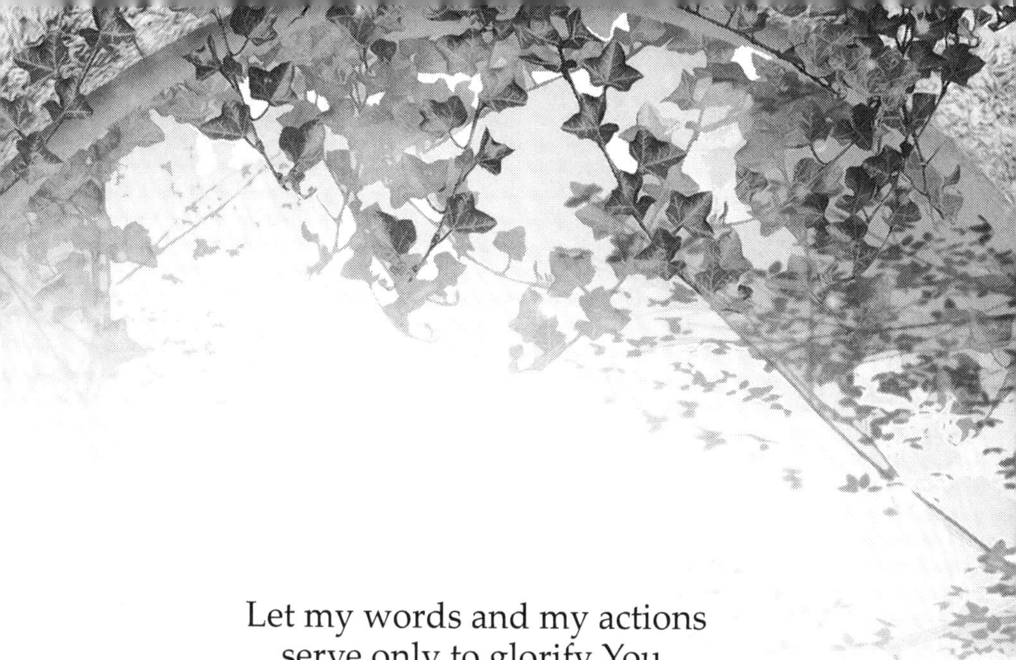

Let my words and my actions
serve only to glorify You.
May they heal and comfort
the lives of those in need.

(Psalm 19:14; Colossians 3:15-17)

In You, Lord, I put my trust.

(Psalm 71:1)

I know that You love me
and supply all my needs,
according to Your riches
in glory by Christ Jesus.

(Philippians 4:19)

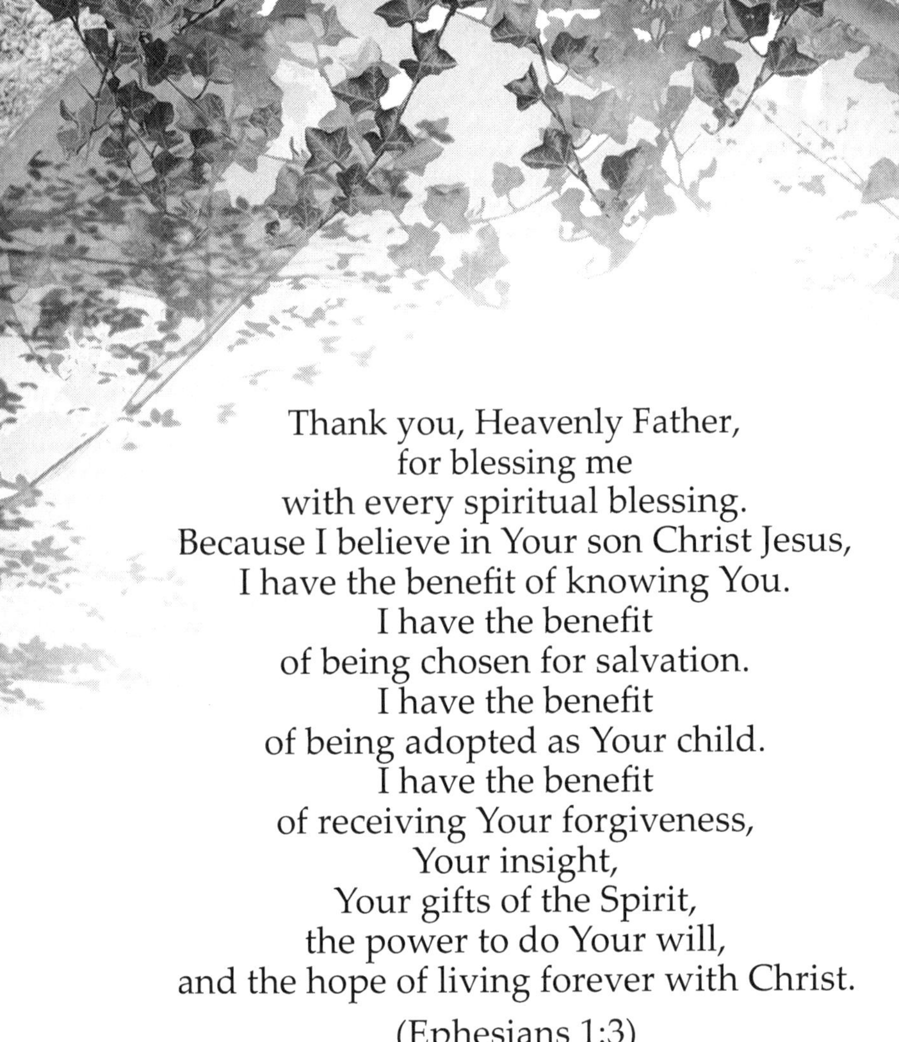

Thank you, Heavenly Father,
for blessing me
with every spiritual blessing.
Because I believe in Your son Christ Jesus,
I have the benefit of knowing You.
I have the benefit
of being chosen for salvation.
I have the benefit
of being adopted as Your child.
I have the benefit
of receiving Your forgiveness,
Your insight,
Your gifts of the Spirit,
the power to do Your will,
and the hope of living forever with Christ.

(Ephesians 1:3)

Strengthen my faith today, Lord,
because without faith,
it is impossible to please You.

(Hebrews 11:6)

Thank you for instructing and teaching me
in the way I should go;
thank you for Your counsel
and for watching over me.

(Psalm 32:8)

In every situation, remind me to ask,
"What Would Jesus Do?"

(Philippians 2:5)

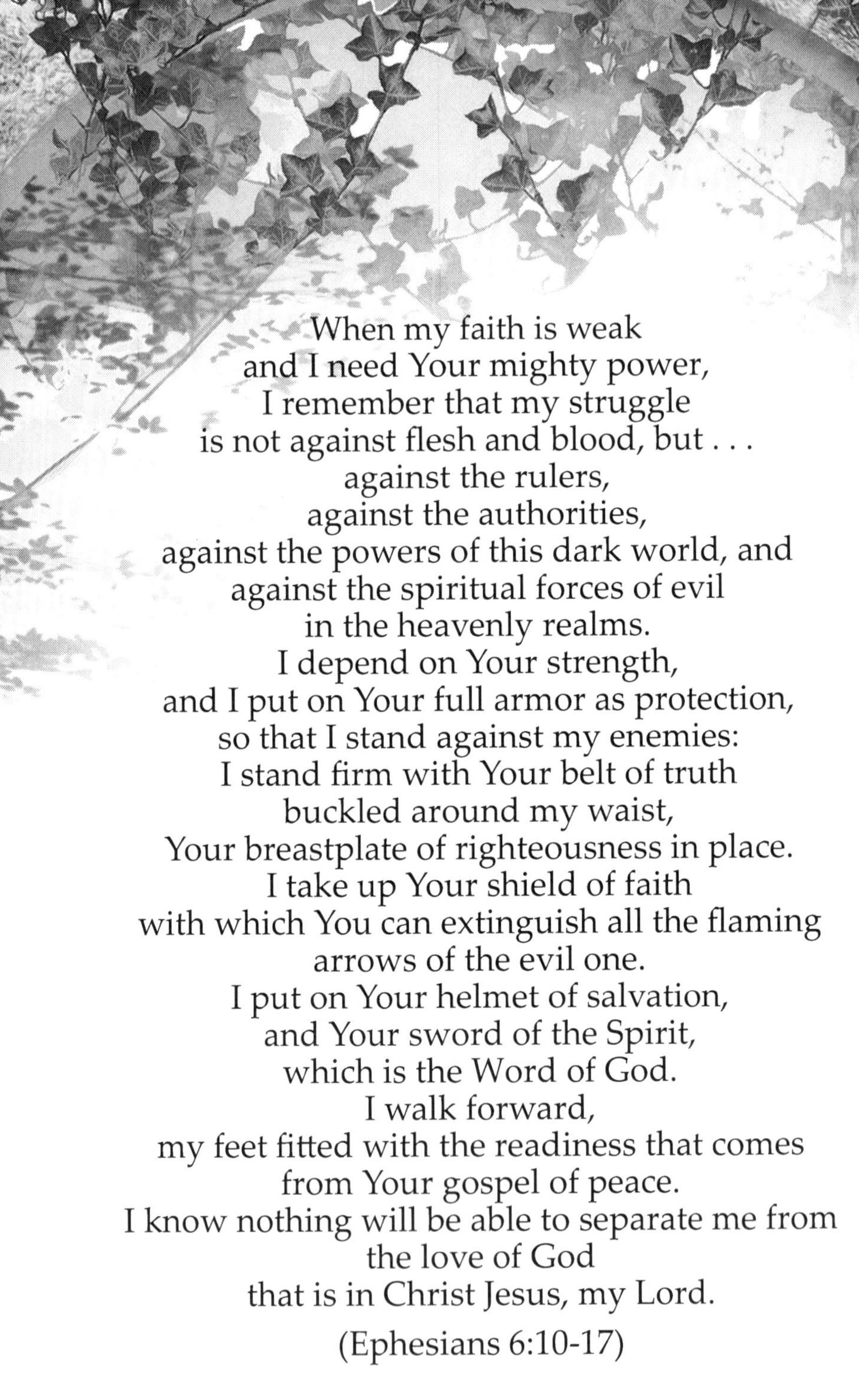

When my faith is weak
and I need Your mighty power,
I remember that my struggle
is not against flesh and blood, but . . .
against the rulers,
against the authorities,
against the powers of this dark world, and
against the spiritual forces of evil
in the heavenly realms.
I depend on Your strength,
and I put on Your full armor as protection,
so that I stand against my enemies:
I stand firm with Your belt of truth
buckled around my waist,
Your breastplate of righteousness in place.
I take up Your shield of faith
with which You can extinguish all the flaming
arrows of the evil one.
I put on Your helmet of salvation,
and Your sword of the Spirit,
which is the Word of God.
I walk forward,
my feet fitted with the readiness that comes
from Your gospel of peace.
I know nothing will be able to separate me from
the love of God
that is in Christ Jesus, my Lord.

(Ephesians 6:10-17)

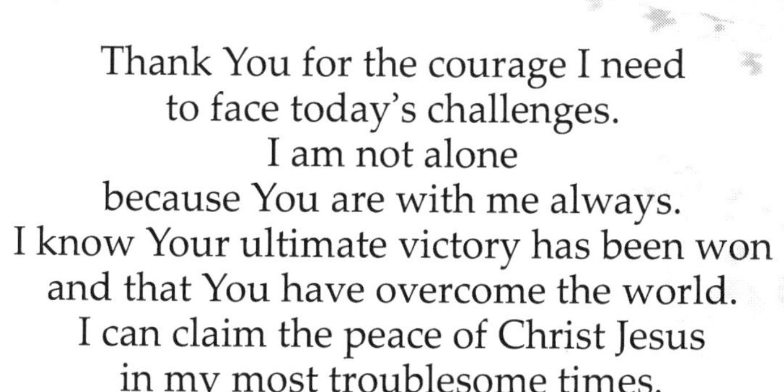

Thank You for the courage I need
to face today's challenges.
I am not alone
because You are with me always.
I know Your ultimate victory has been won
and that You have overcome the world.
I can claim the peace of Christ Jesus
in my most troublesome times.

(1 John 5:4)

Because Your power is a present reality,
I am diligently growing
as a believer in Christ Jesus,
adding to my faith the characteristics of
virtue, goodness, courage, knowledge,
discernment of true from false teaching,
self-control in the face of temptation,
and perseverance amid difficulties.
Help me to always show brotherly kindness
and demonstrate love to all people.

(2 Peter 1:5-7)

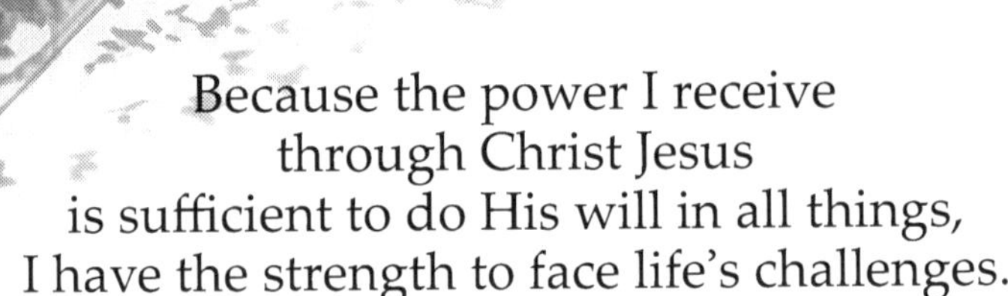

Because the power I receive
through Christ Jesus
is sufficient to do His will in all things,
I have the strength to face life's challenges.

(Philippians 4:13)

O, Lord, You are my shepherd;
You give me all that I need.
You give me a place to rest in green meadows;
You lead me beside peaceful streams.
You renew my strength.
You guide me along the righteous paths
that bring honor to Your name.
Even when I walk through the darkest valley,
I will not be afraid for you are close beside me,
holding my hand.
Your rod and your staff protect and comfort me.
You prepare a feast for me
in the presence of my enemies.
You honor me by anointing my head with oil.
My cup overflows with many blessings.
Your goodness and unfailing love
will be with me all the days of my life,
and I will spend eternity with You.

(Psalm 23)

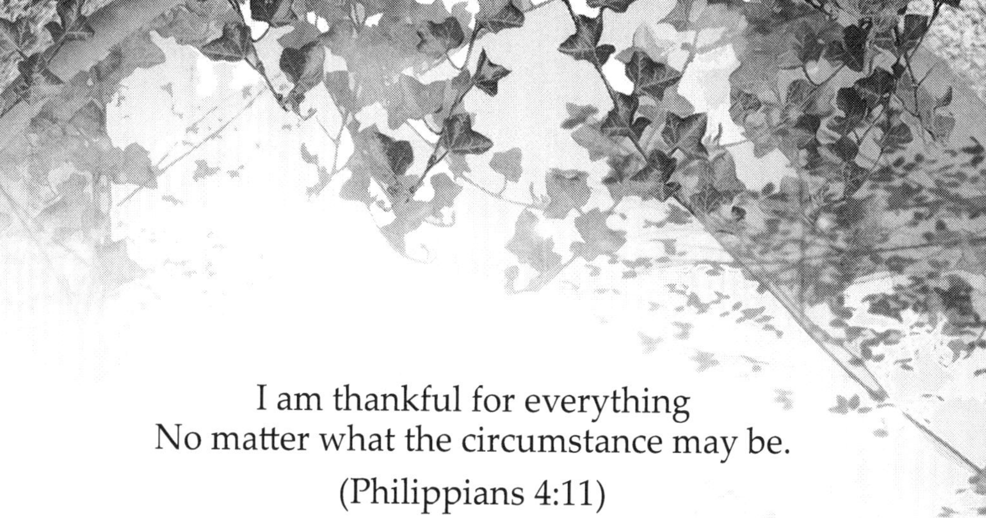

I am thankful for everything
No matter what the circumstance may be.

(Philippians 4:11)

Whatever things are True,
Whatever things are Noble,
Whatever things are Just,
Whatever things are Pure,
Whatever things are Lovely,
Whatever things are Admirable,
Virtuous and Praiseworthy…
I will meditate on these things.

(Philippians 4:8)

I am diligent to present myself approved to You
as a worker who is not ashamed
when You examine my work.

(2 Timothy 2:15)

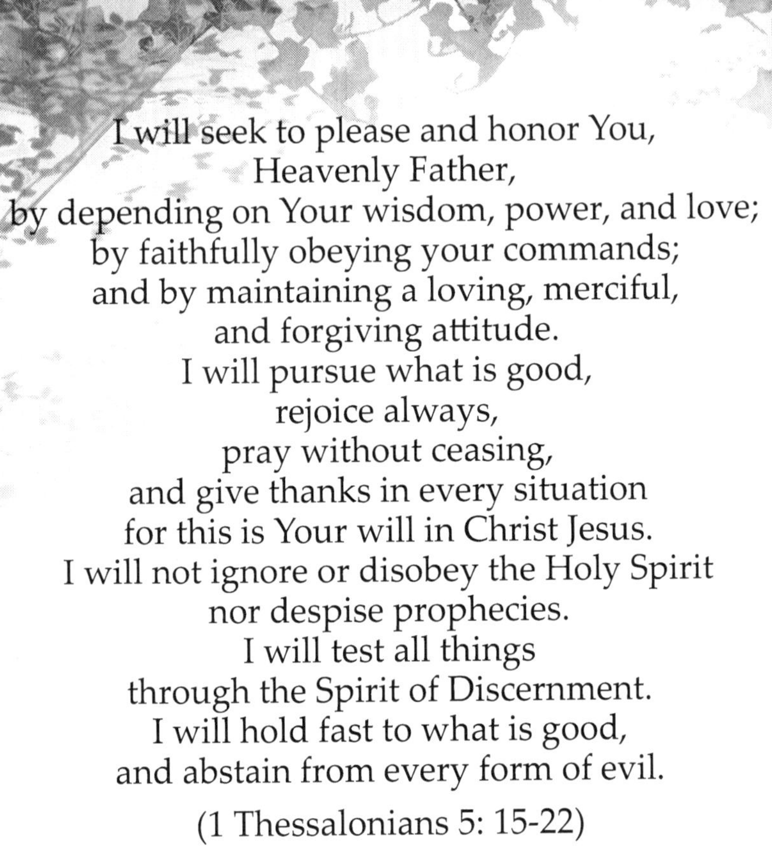

I will seek to please and honor You,
Heavenly Father,
by depending on Your wisdom, power, and love;
by faithfully obeying your commands;
and by maintaining a loving, merciful,
and forgiving attitude.
I will pursue what is good,
rejoice always,
pray without ceasing,
and give thanks in every situation
for this is Your will in Christ Jesus.
I will not ignore or disobey the Holy Spirit
nor despise prophecies.
I will test all things
through the Spirit of Discernment.
I will hold fast to what is good,
and abstain from every form of evil.

(1 Thessalonians 5: 15-22)

I know that in all things
You work to turn every circumstance around
for my spiritual good
because I love you,
and I have been called
according to Your purpose.

(Romans 8:28)

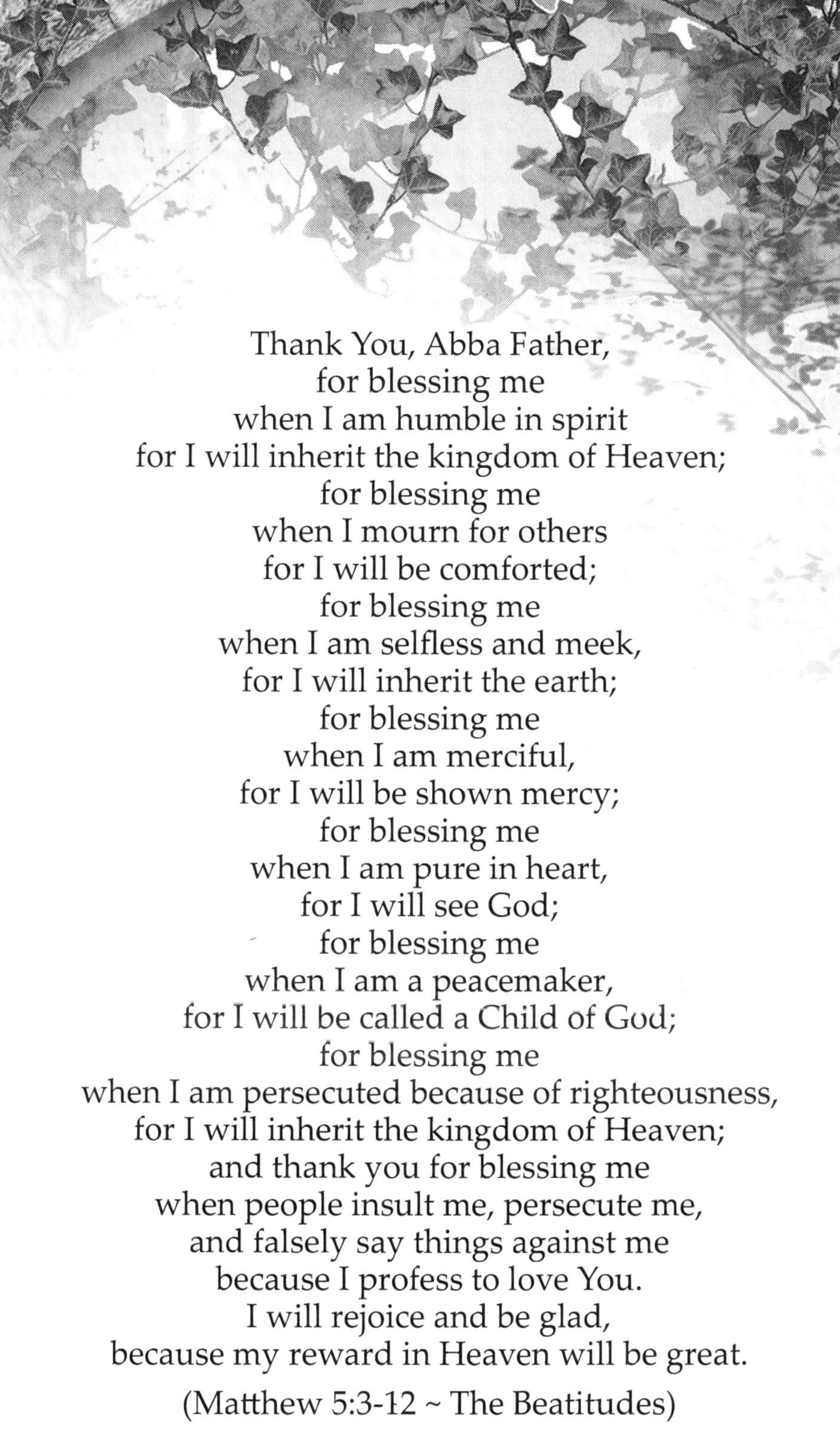

Thank You, Abba Father,
for blessing me
when I am humble in spirit
for I will inherit the kingdom of Heaven;
for blessing me
when I mourn for others
for I will be comforted;
for blessing me
when I am selfless and meek,
for I will inherit the earth;
for blessing me
when I am merciful,
for I will be shown mercy;
for blessing me
when I am pure in heart,
for I will see God;
for blessing me
when I am a peacemaker,
for I will be called a Child of God;
for blessing me
when I am persecuted because of righteousness,
for I will inherit the kingdom of Heaven;
and thank you for blessing me
when people insult me, persecute me,
and falsely say things against me
because I profess to love You.
I will rejoice and be glad,
because my reward in Heaven will be great.

(Matthew 5:3-12 ~ The Beatitudes)

I exalt You, O Lord.
You are my passion, my purpose for living.
Without You, I am nothing but an empty shell.

(Psalm 34:3)

You are my sovereign God.
Anoint me. Use me.
I'm available for Your glory.
I seek to be true to You, Father God,
true to myself, and true to others.
Teach me to always be authentic.

(Psalm 25:21, Psalm 7:8)

I worship You, Heavenly Father,
expressing my praise and thanksgiving
through grateful declarations
and joyful singing of hymns.

(Hebrews 13:15)

Help me, Lord, to be very careful
as to how I live each day,
making the most of every opportunity,
keeping my standards high,
acting wisely, and doing good whenever I can.

(Ephesians 5:15-16)

I hunger and thirst for Your righteousness.
I want my life to reflect Your glory.

(Matthew 5:6)

I abide in You, and you abide in me.
As the branch cannot bear fruit of itself
unless it abides in the vine,
so neither can I, unless I abide in You.
You are the vine, and I am the branch.
As long as I abide in You,
and You abide in me,
I can bear much fruit.
Apart from You,
I can do nothing.

(John 15:4-5)

Heavenly Father,
may Your name be kept holy,
for You are my holy God.
May Your kingdom come soon.
Let Your will be done on earth
as it is in Heaven.
Thank you for the food
that I receive from you daily.
Please forgive my sins, as I have forgiven those
who have sinned against me.
Keep me from the many temptations
that surround me,
and rescue me from the evil one.
Yours is the kingdom and the power
and the glory forever.
Amen

(Matthew 6:9-13)

The greatest achievement
I can accomplish in my life
is to live for Your glory.
Thank You for this time of prayer,
a Holy time within Your Sanctuary,
a time of worship, praise, and thanksgiving;
a time of lying down
and resting in your green meadows;
a time of being led beside your still
and calming streams,
and a time of restoring my soul.
Thank You for Your Sanctuary within me,
where You live.

(Psalm 23:2-3)

Section III
Sanctuary
Prayer

7

Praying in Your Sanctuary

When you pray, go into your room
[your Sanctuary],
and when you have shut your door,
pray to your Heavenly Father
who is in the secret place;
and your Father who sees in secret
will reward you openly.

~ Matthew 6:6[1]

Talking with your Heavenly Father when you are alone with Him in your Sanctuary is like spending time with your closest friend. God first initiated this friendship; how we respond to Him gives an added dimension to the relationship. Yes, He is not only someone with whom you share your deepest concerns—He is also your holy, magnificent, awesome, loving, and living God who deserves your highest praise and honor. This is the ultimate relationship and is unlike any other you have ever experienced.

We do not come to God in prayer to win His favor or love for us. God has already shown us His love through His son Christ Jesus who died for our sins and transgressions. Rather, prayer is the most intimate form of communion with God; it shows Him that we desire a personal union with Him.

Prayer is turning our hearts heavenward, focusing on Him, listening to His voice, and surrendering to His will for our lives. Yielding ourselves in submission to Him is necessary to be able to hear his voice. This is not a passive exercise but, rather, it is an active choice displayed out of strength, not weakness. We choose to surrender and say, "Not my will, but your will." We choose to be in His will.

> Prayer is the energy and life of the soul. By prayer all storm clouds are driven away, mountains of discouragement are cast into the sea, chasms of difficulties are bridged, hope is given wings, faith increases, and joys abound. Hell may rage and threaten, but he who is frequent and fervent in prayer experiences no alarm. By prayer, the windows of heaven are opened, and showers of refreshing dews are rained upon the soul. It is as a watered garden, a fertile spot where blooms the unfading rose of Sharon and the lily of the valley; where spread the undecaying, unwithering branches of the tree of life.[2]

Your time alone with God begins with confessing your sins and asking Him to forgive those sins. Since the blood of Christ Jesus cleanses you from all unrighteousness, confession and cleansing prepares you to enter into His Sanctuary and experience the ultimate relationship.

Effective Prayer

To pray more effectively, you may want to *ask the Holy Spirit to help you.* Why? Because the Spirit "helps us in our weakness; for we do not know what prayers to offer nor in what way to offer them. But the Spirit Himself pleads for us in yearnings that can find no words" (Romans 8:26). So you can ask the Holy Spirit to pray for you, especially in times of deep need where no human words seem to convey what your own spirit wants to say.

The Holy Spirit also helps you in prayer by speaking to you as you meditate on Scripture and the affirmations. John 16:13 says that the Holy Spirit "will guide you into all the truth; for He will not speak on His own initiative, but whatever He hears, He will speak; and He will disclose to you what is to come."

Praying effectively also involves *thanking God for all He has done for you and praising Him for who He is.* Gratitude and praise increases your faith and helps to keep your focus on God's greatness and power. Psalm 100:4 tells us to "enter into His gates with thanksgiving, and into His courts with praise. Be thankful to Him, and bless His name." So let's try to do that as we enter the gates of our sanctuary.

Of course, *spending time worshiping and adoring your Heavenly Father* deepens your relationship with Him. In his book *Let the Nations Be Glad*, John Piper writes, "Worship is essentially an inner stirring of the heart to treasure God above all the treasures of the world."[3]

Prayer Requests

After preparing your heart and spirit for effective prayer, you'll naturally want to *ask God for your specific needs.* Psalm 37:4 says that if you delight yourselves in the Lord, He will give you the desires of your heart.

Pray that although you have specific wants and desires, God will accomplish His will in your life. Have faith, believing that God answers prayers. It may not be within your time frame or in quite the way you would desire, but know that God wants the very best for His children. So the manner in which He answers your prayers will be for your highest good.

Pray also that *God will reveal all the areas in your life that you need to work on* so that you can be the very best you can be in His service.

Then, *thank God for the answers to your prayers, both before and after you see the results.* Philippians 4:6-7 tells us not to worry about anything; instead, pray about everything. Tell God what you need, and thank Him for all He has done. Then you will experience God's peace, which exceeds anything we can understand. His peace will guard your hearts and minds as you live in Christ Jesus.

Is there a right way to direct prayers and petitions to our Holy Father?

No, but Jesus emphasized that we should pray with faith and simplicity. Our prayers can be long or very short. But Jesus instructs us in Matthew 6:7 how *not* to pray:

> When you pray, do not use vain repetitions as
> the heathen do. For they think they will be heard
> for their many words.

Then Jesus tells us how to pray in Matthew 6:9-14:

> Our Father in heaven, hallowed be Your name.
> Your kingdom come,
> Your will be done on earth as it is in heaven.
> Give us this day our daily bread.
> And forgive our sins as we forgive
> those who sin against us.
> And do not lead us into temptation,
> but deliver us from the evil one.
> For Yours is the kingdom and the power
> and the glory forever.
> Amen.

This Lord's prayer (as it is often called) is not to be repeated by rote memory. Every part of it—His hallowed name, His kingdom, His provision, His forgiveness, and our duty to forgive—provides a guide to understanding what God wants us to focus on in our own prayers. So pray this Lord's prayer slowly, meditating on each word and phrase. You learned how to do this when we discussed how to pray through your affirmations in chapter 5.

Participate in God's Promises

If you ever feel like your prayer time doesn't matter to God, remind yourself (by reading the Scriptures below) of how much God wants you to participate in prayer with him. Remind yourself, too, that He promises to respond, but He needs you to take the initiative.

Whatever things you ask in prayer believing,
you will receive.

- Matthew 21:22 (NKJV)

Ask and it will be given to you;
seek, and you will find;
knock, and the door will be opened to you.
For everyone who asks receives;
and he who seeks finds,
and to him who knocks,
the door will be opened.

- Matthew 7:7-8 (NKJV)

You do not have,
because you do not ask (God).

- James 4:2 (NKJV)

Be anxious for nothing,
but in everything by prayer and supplication,
with thanksgiving, let your requests
be made known to God;
and the peace of God,
which surpasses all understanding,
will guard your hearts and minds
through Christ Jesus.

~ Philippians 4:6~7 (NKJV)

God shall supply all your needs,
according to His riches
in glory by Christ Jesus.

~ Philippians 4:19 (NKJV)

In the morning,
O Lord, you hear my voice;
in the morning
I lay my requests before you
and wait in expectation.

~ Psalm 5:3

All things for which you pray and ask,
believe that you have received them,
and they will be granted you.

~ Mark 11:24 (NASB)

When you are praying,
first forgive anyone
you are holding a grudge against,
so that your Father in heaven
will forgive your sins, too.

~ Mark 11:25 (paraphrased)

If I have iniquity (sin) in my heart,
the Lord will not hear me.

~ Psalm 66:18 (paraphrased)

Call to Me and I will answer you,
and I will tell you great and mighty things,
which you do not know.

~ Jeremiah 33:3 (NKJV)

If my people, who are called by my name,
will humble themselves, pray, search for me,
and turn from their evil ways,
then I will hear their prayers,
and forgive their sins.

- 2 Chronicles 7:14 (paraphrased)

It is impossible to please God without faith.
Anyone who wants to come to Him
must believe that God exists
and that He rewards those
who sincerely seek Him.

- Hebrews 11:6 (NLT)

But he must ask in faith,
without any doubts,
for the one who has doubts
is like a wave of the sea
that is driven and tossed by the wind.

- James 1:6 (ISV 2008)

All things are possible for one who believes.

- Mark 9:23 (ESV)

Seek the Lord your God, and you will find Him
if you search for Him with all your heart
and all your soul.
When you are in distress,
return to the Lord your God
and listen to His voice.
For the Lord your God is a compassionate God;
He will not fail you.

- Deuteronomy 4:29-31 (NASB)

Pray without ceasing.

- 1 Thessalonians 5:17 (ESV)

What Does It Mean to Pray in the Name of Jesus?

> Christ Jesus said, "I tell you with certainty, whatever you ask the Father for ***in my name***, He will give it to you."
>
> - John 16:23

The above words of Jesus mean that we should pray according to the will of God. Praying in Jesus' name is praying for the things that will honor and glorify Christ Jesus. It's the understanding that our prayers are heard as we approach His throne of grace.

Naturally, only those who believe that the Lord Christ Jesus died and rose from the grave and lives in Heaven with the Father where He intercedes for us can pray in Jesus' name. If we truly believe that, we can be confident that He will listen to us whenever we ask Him for anything in line with His will. And if we know He is listening when we make our requests, we can be sure that He will give us what we ask for (see 1 John 5:14-15).

Christ Jesus said again in John 14:13-14: "You can ask for anything in my name, and I will do it, because the work of the Son brings glory to the Father. Yes, ask anything in my name, and I will do it!" And the apostle Paul reminds us to "always give thanks for everything to God the Father in the name of our Lord Jesus Christ" (Ephesians 5:20). So if Jesus said it and Paul said, let us do it.

Examples of Prayer Requests

The following are examples of prayers that you can start with as you grow in your own prayer time with your Father:

Abba Father,

Thank you for my family, my home, my job.

Forgive me for my sins of ________________ and for those that are unknown. Teach me to be more obedient to Your will. Give me the understanding of the power of prayer and the knowledge of the hope that is in Christ Jesus.

I ask this in Jesus' name, Amen

Thank you, Heavenly Father, for all the many blessings You have given me. Renew the spirit of my mind. Let Your love and light flow through me so that I may be a blessing to others.

In Jesus' precious name, I pray.

Amen

Abba Father,

You are so good; you are so wonderful. I am aware that I need more of Your grace. I am ashamed that I have neglected you. O God, I want to want You more each day; I want to be filled with longing for you. Show me Your glory, so that I may know you intimately. Begin a new work of love within me. Give me the grace to follow You, even when I question You.

In Jesus' name, I pray.

Amen

Lord,

Help me to live today, like I wish I had lived in the past. Make me into the person you created me to be before I got in the way.

In Jesus' name.

Amen.

Heavenly Father,

I bring my prayer requests before you. You are the Great Physician, the Almighty Healer. If it is your will, I ask that you heal ____________, that you comfort him and surround him with your love. If he does not know you as his personal Savior and Lord, I ask that you speak to him, and let him know that he needs you in his life now.

In Jesus' name.

Amen.

Our Father in Heaven,

You know my needs without my having to say them, but I could really use your help right now. . . . Help me to listen quietly and to hear your answers.

In Jesus' Precious Name.

Amen.

8

Prayer Request Journal

Whatever things you ask in prayer believing,
you will receive.

~ Matthew 21:22

Your personal prayers can be written on the following pages or by making your own Prayer Request Journal. Writing your prayer requests is an ideal way to help you focus on your needs and the needs of others and to keep track of how God answers your prayers.

You may want to organize the pages so that you have a section for your needs and desires, another for your family, another for your friends, another for your spiritual leaders, another for your country and its leaders, and so on.

Prayer Requests

Date: ____________________

I prayed for . . .

Prayers Answered

Date: ____________________

God answered my prayer in this way . . .

Prayer Requests

Date: ____________________

I prayed for . . .

Prayers Answered

Date: ____________________

God answered my prayer in this way . . .

Prayer Requests

Date: ______________________

I prayed for . . .

____
____
____
____
____
____
____
____
____

Prayers Answered

Date: ______________________

God answered my prayer in this way . . .

____
____
____
____
____
____
____
____

Prayer Requests

Date: ______________________

I prayed for . . .

____

____

____

____

____

____

____

____

____

Prayers Answered

Date: ______________________

God answered my prayer in this way . . .

____

____

____

____

____

____

____

____

Prayer Requests

Date: ____________

I prayed for . . .

Prayers Answered

Date: ____________

God answered my prayer in this way . . .

Prayer Requests

Date: ______________________

I prayed for . . .

Prayers Answered

Date: ______________________

God answered my prayer in this way . . .

Date: ____________________

I prayed for . . .

Prayers Answered

Date: ____________________

God answered my prayer in this way . . .

Prayer Requests

Date: ____________________

I prayed for . . .

Prayers Answered

Date: ____________________

God answered my prayer in this way . . .

Prayer Requests

Date: ____________________

I prayed for . . .

____

____

____

____

____

____

____

____

____

Prayers Answered

Date: ____________________

God answered my prayer in this way . . .

____

____

____

____

____

____

____

____

Prayer Requests

Date: ____________________

I prayed for . . .

Prayers Answered

Date: ____________________

God answered my prayer in this way . . .

Prayer Requests

Date: ____________________

I prayed for . . .

Prayers Answered

Date: ____________________

God answered my prayer in this way . . .

Prayer Requests

Date: ____________________

I prayed for . . .

Prayers Answered

Date: ____________________

God answered my prayer in this way . . .

Prayer Requests

Date: ____________________

I prayed for . . .

Prayers Answered

Date: ____________________

God answered my prayer in this way . . .

Prayer Requests

Date: ____________________

I prayed for . . .

Prayers Answered

Date: ____________________

God answered my prayer in this way . . .

Prayer Requests

Date:

I prayed for . . .

Prayers Answered

Date:

God answered my prayer in this way . . .

Prayer Requests

Date: ____________________

I prayed for . . .

Prayers Answered

Date: ____________________

God answered my prayer in this way . . .

Prayer Requests

Date: ____________________

I prayed for . . .

Prayers Answered

Date: ____________________

God answered my prayer in this way . . .

Prayer Requests

Date: ______________________

I prayed for . . .

Prayers Answered

Date: ______________________

God answered my prayer in this way . . .

Prayer Requests

Date: ________________

I prayed for . . .

Prayers Answered

Date: ________________

God answered my prayer in this way . . .

Prayer Requests

Date:

I prayed for . . .

Prayers Answered

Date:

God answered my prayer in this way . . .

Prayer Requests

Date: ____________________

I prayed for . . .

Prayers Answered

Date: ____________________

God answered my prayer in this way . . .

Prayer Requests

Date: ____________________

I prayed for . . .

Prayers Answered

Date: ____________________

God answered my prayer in this way . . .

Prayer Requests

Date: ____________________

I prayed for . . .

Prayers Answered

Date: ____________________

God answered my prayer in this way . . .

Prayer Requests

Date: ______________________

I prayed for . . .

Prayers Answered

Date: ______________________

God answered my prayer in this way . . .

Section IV
Devotional Journal

Date:

Date:

Date: ____________________

Date: ____________________

Date:

Date:

Date: ____________________

Date:

Date: ______________________

Date:

Date: ____________________

Date:

Date: ______________________

Date:

Date: ____________________

Date:

Date: ______________________

Date: ____________________

Date:

Date:

Date: ____________________

Date: ______________________

Notes

Page xi

1. Charles Ebert Orr, *Food for the Lambs,* (in public domain, re-released by Project Gutenberg, 2004) available at www.gutenberg.org/ebooks/13294

Alone with God

1. Words by Johnson Oatman, Jr., Music by William J. Kirkpatrick (c.1904)

Talking with God

1. Adapted from Amplified Bible

Chapter One

1. Adapted from Amplified Bible

Chapter Two

1. Charles Ebert Orr, *Food for the Lambs*
2. Written by Gospel singer, Thomas A. Dorsey
3. Quoted from NASB
4. Quoted from NLT
5. Orr, *Food for the Lambs*

Chapter Three

1. Penned by hymnist Horatio Spafford after a series of traumatic losses in his life. Melody composed by Philip Bliss.

2. Frederick William Faber, "Spiritual Conferences" (Dublin: Thomas Richardson and Son, 1860), 408.

Chapter Four

1. Adapted from Scripture

2. Written by Austin Miles (1912)

Chapter Seven

1. Adapted from Scripture

2. Orr, *Food for the Lambs*

3. John Piper, *Let the Nations Be Glad,* (Grand Rapids: Baker Academic, 2010), 231.

About Gi Gi Griffin

Gi Gi Griffin grew up as an only child in a Christian home in the Midwest. For the first ten years of her life, she traveled extensively with her parents as they ministered in music to churches of all denominations. As a small child, Gi Gi sang solos in her parents' concerts.

While in the University of Colorado, Gi Gi enrolled as a music education major, hoping to eventually become a singer and stage actor in musical comedies. In high school and college she worked as a professional fashion model before moving to Los Angeles to work in the fashion industry.

For over 25 years, Gi Gi was a sales representative for several manufacturers of fine women's apparel, including Kimberly Knitwear, St. John Knits, and David Hayes Couture. She traveled nationwide, presenting trunk shows and fashion shows in exclusive retail stores.

Since 1992, Gi Gi Griffin has been a full-time Realtor in the beautiful South Bay/Palos Verdes area in Southern California.

Gi Gi has been blessed to be a long-time member of Rolling Hills Covenant Church under the teachings of its Christ-centered pastoral staff who have inspired her to stay on the path into God's Sanctuary and help others do the same.

She is married to Alfred Griffin and they have no children, except for their four-legged kids—their Shetland Sheepdogs Lily and Joy.

Made in the USA
San Bernardino, CA
18 October 2016